READING POWER

Famous American Trails

The Santa Fe Trail

From Independence, Missouri, to Santa Fe, New Mexico

Arlan Dean

The Rosen Publishing Group's
PowerKids Press™
New York

Published in 2003 by The Rosen Publishing Group, Inc.
29 East 21st Street, New York, NY 10010

First Edition

Book Design: Christopher Logan

Photo Credits: Cover © North Wind Picture Archives; pp. 4–5 © Hulton/Archive/Getty Images; p. 5 (inset) Christopher Logan; pp. 6–7, 10, 17 (inset), 18–19 Denver Public Library, Western History Collection (X-9216, X-22266, X-32213, X-32246); p. 7 (inset) Missouri Historical Society, St. Louis; pp. 8–9 © Academy of Natural Sciences of Philadelphia/Corbis; p. 11 © Corbis; pp. 12, 20 courtesy, Colorado Historical Society, (C. Waldo Love, CHS-X3303; William Henry Jackson, CHS-J2428); p. 13 © Buddy Mays/Corbis; pp. 14–15 courtesy Peter E. Palmquist Collection; pp. 16–17 courtesy American Heritage Center, University of Wyoming; p. 16 (inset) courtesy of the Burton Historical Collection, Detroit Public Library; p. 19 (inset) © Michael T. Sedam/Corbis; p. 21 © Tom Bean/Corbis

Library of Congress Cataloging-in-Publication Data

Dean, Arlan.
The Santa Fe Trail : from Independence, Missouri to Santa Fe, New Mexico / Arlan Dean.
   v. cm. — (Famous American trails)
Includes bibliographical references and index.
Contents: The Louisiana Purchase — Santa Fe — The traders — Dangerous trail — End of the line.
ISBN 0-8239-6481-7 (lib. bdg.)
1. Santa Fe National Historic Trail—Juvenile literature. 2. Southwest, New—History—Juvenile literature. [1. Santa Fe National Historic Trail. 2. Southwest, New—History.] I. Title.
F786 .D386 2003
978'.02—dc21

                                                    2002002937

Contents

The Santa Fe Trail

In the early 1800s, many Americans wanted to travel to the West to trade goods. The Santa Fe Trail was one of the main trails used by traders.

Traders on the Santa Fe Trail often set up camp by forming a circle with their wagons. Sometimes soldiers helped guard the traders' camp.

The trail began in Independence, Missouri. It went through parts of Kansas, Colorado, and Oklahoma before ending in Santa Fe in the present-day state of New Mexico. The trail was about 780 miles long.

THE SANTA FE TRAIL

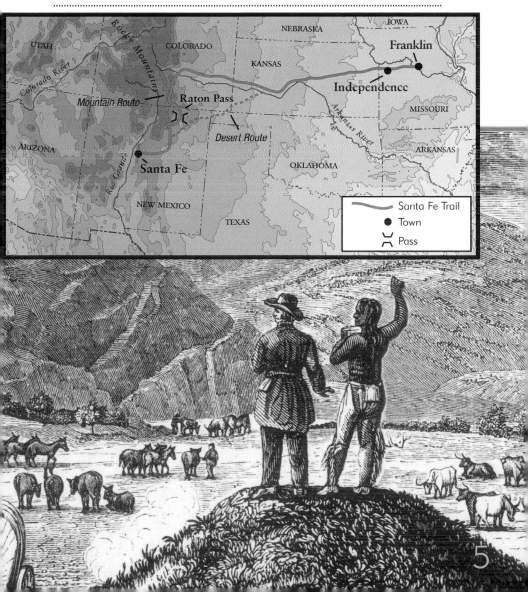

Opening the Santa Fe Trail

William Becknell opened the Santa Fe Trail in 1821. Becknell and a group of five men began their travels in Franklin, Missouri, and followed the Arkansas River west to the Rocky Mountains.

The Santa Fe Trail went through land that was very rocky and had many mountains.

Then, they turned south and crossed the mountains at Raton Pass. This part of the trail later became known as the Mountain Route.

Franklin, Missouri, was the first starting point of the Santa Fe Trail. After a flood destroyed Franklin in 1828, the trail's starting point was moved to Independence, Missouri (pictured).

On his second trip to Santa Fe, Becknell wanted to take lots of goods to trade or sell. He filled wagons with his trade goods. However, he knew the wagons were too big to travel through Raton Pass.

The Desert Route was 100 miles shorter than the Mountain Route. Part of the route was a 50-mile stretch of desert where there was no water. Comanches often attacked wagon trains along this route. This picture shows a traveler crossing a desert near the Desert Route.

Becknell and his group of 22 men took a new route to Santa Fe. This route passed south of the Rocky Mountains and went through a desert. It became known as the Desert Route.

Taking Goods to the West

By the mid-1820s, many traders used wagons to take their goods to Santa Fe. There, they traded their goods for burros, horses, furs, gold, and silver.

Some traders used mules to carry their goods to Santa Fe. Mules were able to carry about 350 pounds of goods and travel 15 miles a day.

The wagons used on the Santa Fe Trail were known as prairie
schooners because they looked like fast-moving sailing ships.

In 1833, William and Charles Bent formed a company that set up a trading fort on the Santa Fe Trail. The fort was built along the Arkansas River near the Rocky Mountains. The trading fort was a place where traders and other travelers could rest, get food, and fix their wagons.

William Bent built a second fort about 40 miles from the first one.

William and Charles Bent also traded with settlers and Native Americans who lived nearby. The Native Americans traded robes made of buffalo skins for knives, pots, and lead.

Today, Bent's Fort is a National Historic Site. The trading fort has been rebuilt to look like it did in 1833. The fort includes a blacksmith shop and a trading post.

Between 1822 and 1843, about 80 wagons and 150 people used the Santa Fe Trail every year. After gold was discovered in California in 1848, more people began to use the trail. By the late 1860s, over 5,000 wagons used the trail every year.

Prospectors used the Santa Fe Trail to get to California to look for gold.

Protecting the Travelers

Travelers using the Santa Fe Trail often hunted buffalo for food. However, many of them killed more buffalo than they needed. Buffalo bones littered the trail and the surrounding lands.

On their way west, travelers killed thousands of buffalo. Here, a man stands on a large pile of buffalo bones.

There were fewer buffalo for the Native Americans to use for food and clothing. Traders and settlers also cut down trees that Native Americans used for fuel and housing.

Native Americans, such as Comanches, needed the buffalo for food and clothing.

The Native Americans became angry with the travelers. Sometimes, they attacked the travelers along the trail. The Santa Fe Trail became unsafe. To protect travelers, the U.S. Army built forts along the trail.

Today, the remains of some of the forts used to protect people using the Santa Fe Trail can still be seen. The buildings in this picture are from Fort Union in New Mexico.

The End of the Trail

By the late 1860s, railroads became the fastest way to move people and goods to the West. In 1879, the railroad reached Santa Fe. Soon, the Santa Fe Trail was no longer used. The Santa Fe Trail played an important part in opening up the West to the rest of the country.

A railroad line that went to Santa Fe was built near the Santa Fe Trail.

The Santa Fe Trail Time Line

1821	*William Becknell opens the Santa Fe Trail.*
1833	*William and Charles Bent form a company that set up a trading fort on the trail.*
1848	*People use the trail to get to California to find gold.*
1860s	*Railroads are being built across the country.*
1879	*The railroad reaches Santa Fe. Soon after, the trail is no longer used.*
1987	*The Santa Fe Trail is made a National Historic Trail.*

Today, stone trail markers show where parts of the Santa Fe Trail were.

Glossary

burros (**ber**-ohz) small donkeys

fuel (**fyoo**-uhl) something that is burned to produce heat or power

goods (**gudz**) things, such as cloth, that are produced for sale

pass (**pas**) a low place in a mountain range

prospectors (**prahs**-pehk-tuhrz) people who search a place for things, such as gold, that will make them rich

route (**root**) a way taken to get somewhere

settlers (**seht**-luhrz) people who come to stay in a new country or place

traders (**tray**-duhrz) people who buy and sell things

trading fort (**trayd**-ihng **fort**) a strong building or place that can be easily guarded and is used as a rest stop for travelers and as a store for trading goods

Resources

Books

The Santa Fe Trail
by Judy Alter
Children's Press (1999)

The Santa Fe Trail
by Jean F. Blashfield
Compass Point Books (2000)

Web Sites

Due to the changing nature of Internet links, PowerKids Press has developed an online list of Web sites related to the subjects of this book. This site is updated regularly. Please use this link to access the list:

http://www.powerkidslinks.com/fat/sant/

Index

Word Count: 502

Note to Librarians, Teachers, and Parents

If reading is a challenge, Reading Power is a solution! Reading Power is perfect for readers who want high-interest subject matter at an accessible reading level. These fact-filled, photo-illustrated books are designed for readers who want straightforward vocabulary, engaging topics, and a manageable reading experience. With clear picture/text correspondence, leveled Reading Power books put the reader in charge. Now readers have the power to get the information they want and the skills they need in a user-friendly format.